Structure & Speaking Practice
Riyadh

Australia • Brazil • Mexico • Singapore • United Kingdom • United States

NATIONAL GEOGRAPHIC
L E A R N I N G

National Geographic Learning,
a Cengage Company

Structure & Speaking Practice, Riyadh

Nancy Douglas and James R. Morgan

Publisher: Sherrise Roehr

Executive Editor: Laura LeDréan

Managing Editor: Jennifer Monaghan

Digital Implementation Manager,
Irene Boixareu

Senior Media Researcher: Leila Hishmeh

Director of Global Marketing: Ian Martin

Regional Sales and National Account
Manager: Andrew O'Shea

Content Project Manager: Ruth Moore

Senior Designer: Lisa Trager

Manufacturing Planner: Mary Beth
Hennebury

Composition: Lumina Datamatics

For permission to use material from this text or product,
submit all requests online at **cengage.com/permissions**
Further permissions questions can be emailed to
permissionrequest@cengage.com

Student Edition: Structure & Speaking Practice, Riyadh
ISBN-13: 978-0-357-13790-1

National Geographic Learning
20 Channel Center Street
Boston, MA 02210
USA

Locate your local office at **international.cengage.com/region**

Visit National Geographic Learning online at **ELTNGL.com**
Visit our corporate website at **www.cengage.com**

Printed in China
Print Number: 01   Print Year: 2019

Photo Credits

SCOPE & SEQUENCE

Unit / Lesson	Video	Vocabulary	Listening

UNIT 1 FOOD p. 2

| LESSON A
What's on the menu?

LESSON B
Eating right | At the Covered Market | * Foods and drinks
coffee, chicken, sandwich

* Tips for being a healthy eater
healthy, energy, junk food | * Ordering food; talking about meals
Listen for details

* Make a smoothie
Make and check predictions
Listen for details
Listen for sequence |

UNIT 2 TIME p. 16

| LESSON A
My routine

LESSON B
Have a good weekend | Late for Work | * Times and daily routines p. 97
What time is it?, It's 9:15; wake up, take a shower, get dressed
* Weekend activities
go to the movies, go for a walk | * What are your plans?
Listen for gist
Listen for details

* Days off
Listen for details |

UNIT 3 SPECIAL OCCASIONS p. 30

| LESSON A
Holidays

LESSON B
Festivals | Ice Music | * Months and holidays
January, February, March

* Festivals
event, take place, attend | * Booking a flight
Listen for numbers and dates

* Autumn festivals
Infer information
Listen for details |

UNIT 4 HOME p. 44

| LESSON A
Rooms

LESSON B
Home design | Small Spaces, Small Ideas | * Rooms, areas, and items in a house
kitchen, living room, yard, window

* Colors and design
red, yellow, green, dark blue | * Renting an apartment
Listen for gist
Listen for details
Listen for numbers
* Green housing
Make and check predictions
Make predictions
Listen for details |

Expansion Activities p. 58

Grammar	Pronunciation	Speaking	Reading	Writing	Communication
* Simple present tense: affirmative and negative statements * Simple present *Yes / No* questions and answers	*And, or*	Talking about likes and dislikes	Two powerful health foods Scan for information Read for details	Write about a favorite food	* **Plan a dinner party** Create a seating chart for guests according to personal information * **Talk about your favorite food** Express agreement and disagreement
* Prepositions of time: *in, on, at, from... to* * Simple present *Wh-* questions	Numbers: stress; *-ty* and *-teen*	Making suggestions	What kind of weekend person are you? Make predictions Check predictions Read for specific information	Make plans	* **Make a schedule and find time to meet with classmates** * **Interview classmates about weekend activities**
* Prepositions of time: *in* and *on* * *When* and *How long* questions	Ordinal numbers: *th* and *t*	Saying you know or don't know something	**Burning Man** Infer information Scan for information Read for details	Write about a festival	* **Talk about holidays and special occasions** * **Give a class presentation about a festival**
* *There is / There are* * *Very / too*	Rising intonation to show surprise	Showing surprise	The power of color Make predictions Check predictions Scan for information	Describe where you live	* **Describe the location of objects in a room** * **Identify and fix problems with a room**

Language Summaries p. 66   Grammar Notes p. 69

1 FOOD

Look at the photo. Answer the questions.

1 Do you know any of these foods?
  What are they?

2 Which ones do you eat?

3 Do you like them?

UNIT GOALS

1 Order food from a menu

2 Talk about foods you like, dislike, and eat often

3 Talk about healthy eating habits

4 Describe your favorite food

A spread of food and spices

Fruit at the Oxford Covered Market

1 VIDEO At the Covered Market

A ▶ 🔁 Watch the video with the sound off. What foods do you see? Tell a partner.

B ▶ Watch the video. Write the food each person doesn't like.

meat	fish	tomatoes

1. Jan _____

2. Richard _____

3. Amy _____

C 🔁 Do you want to go to Oxford Covered Market? Why or why not? Is there a market like Oxford Covered Market where you live? Tell a partner.

2 VOCABULARY

A With a partner, think of a few fruits and vegetables in English. Do you like to eat any of these items? Share your ideas with the class.

B Look at the pictures and the list of drinks. Ask and answer the questions with a partner.

1. Do you ever eat or drink any of these items?
2. Which ones do you like?
3. What other foods and drinks do you like?

steak **and** baked potato

spinach salad **with** tomatoes **and** onions

cheese **and** fruit

spaghetti **and** tomato sauce

vegetable soup **and** bread

rice **and** beans

fried chicken

tuna sandwich

Common drinks
coffee
milk
orange juice
soda
tea

3 LISTENING

A 🔄 What restaurants do you like? What do you order there? Tell a partner.

B 🔊 **Listen for details.** Mia and Leo are at a restaurant for lunch. Listen. Circle the items that they order from the bills to the right. Then answer the questions. **Track 1**

1. Which person eats in the restaurant ("for here")?

   _____

2. Which person eats out of the restaurant ("to go")?

   _____

C 🔊 🔄 **Pronunciation: *And, or.*** Listen and complete each conversation with the word *and* or *or*. Notice how *and* and *or* are pronounced. Then practice the conversations with a partner. **Track 2**

1. A: Umm… I'd like the spaghetti with tomato sauce.
   B: OK, that comes with soup _____ salad.

2. A: I'd like a chicken sandwich.
   B: OK, that comes with French fries _____ mixed vegetables.

3. A: What juices do you have?
   B: Apple _____ orange.

4. A: Is that for here _____ to go?
   B: For here.

D 🔄 With a partner, order your lunch from the items in **B**. Use the words for ordering food and talking about meals to help you.

Word Bank
Ordering food
What can I get you? / Would you like anything to drink?
I'd like a soup and salad, please. / Orange juice, please.
Talking about meals
breakfast (morning), *lunch* (afternoon), *dinner* (evening)
I <u>have</u> eggs and coffee <u>for</u> breakfast.

Date	Server	For here	Order No
		To go	**0142**

NO		AMOUNT
	MAIN DISHES	
	Chicken sandwich	
	Rice and beans	
	Spaghetti	
	Veggie burger	
	SIDE DISHES	
	Soup	
	Salad	
	French fries	
	Mixed vegetables	
	DRINKS	
	Soda	
	Coffee	
	Bottled water	
	Apple juice	
	Orange juice	
	TAX	

Mia's order

Date	Server	For here	Order No
		To go	**0143**

NO		AMOUNT
	MAIN DISHES	
	Chicken sandwich	
	Rice and beans	
	Spaghetti	
	Veggie burger	
	SIDE DISHES	
	Soup	
	Salad	
	French fries	
	Mixed vegetables	
	DRINKS	
	Soda	
	Coffee	
	Bottled water	
	Apple juice	
	Orange juice	
	TAX	

Leo's order

4 SPEAKING

A 🔊 ⟳ Listen to the conversation and practice it with a partner. Then answer the questions. **Track 3**

1. What can you eat at Tapeo 39?

2. What is perfect for summer? Why?

JASON: I'm hungry.

MARIA: Me, too. Do you like Indian food?

JASON: No, not really.

MARIA: How about Spanish food? I know a fun place.

JASON: Yeah? What is it?

MARIA: It's called Tapeo 39, and they have great gazpacho there.

JASON: What's gazpacho?

MARIA: It's a delicious kind of soup. I like it a lot.

JASON: It's too hot for soup, Maria!

MARIA: Don't worry. It's a cold soup. It's perfect for summer.

JASON: What's in it?

MARIA: Tomatoes, cucumbers, onions, and pepper.

JASON: Sounds good.

MARIA: It is. Oh, and they also have tasty sandwiches.

JASON: Let's go!

Gazpacho

SPEAKING STRATEGY

B Think of two restaurants. Write the information.

Restaurant name: _____   Restaurant name: _____

Kind of food: _____   Kind of food: _____

Food on the menu: _____   Food on the menu: _____

C ⟳ Make new conversations with your partner. Use the conversation in **A** and your information from **B**, as well as the Useful Expressions, to help you.

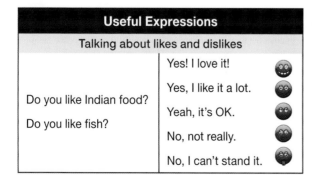

Useful Expressions		
Talking about likes and dislikes		
Do you like Indian food? Do you like fish?	Yes! I love it!	😄
	Yes, I like it a lot.	🙂
	Yeah, it's OK.	😐
	No, not really.	🙁
	No, I can't stand it.	😖

Hey, Pablo, I'm hungry.

I'm hungry, too. I know a great place for dinner. Do you like Chinese food?

5 GRAMMAR

A Turn to page 69. Complete the exercises. Then do **B** and **C** below.

Simple Present Affirmative Statements		
Subject pronoun	**Verb**	
I / You / We / They	eat	meat.
He / She / It	eats	

Simple Present Negative Statements			
Subject pronoun	**do + not**	**Verb**	
I / You / We / They	don't	eat	meat.
He / She / It	doesn't		

B 🔁 Use the verbs in the box to complete the facts about Sylvie. You will use some words more than once. Check your answers with a partner.

do	drink	eat	go	know	study

Sylvie	You
For breakfast, she…	For breakfast, I…
1. _____ a glass of orange juice. But she (not) _____ coffee. She can't stand it.	1. _____
	2. (not) _____
2. _____ eggs and toast. They're her favorite.	_____
After school, she sometimes…	After school, I sometimes…
3. _____ to a cafe and _____ her homework.	3. _____ and _____ my homework.
4. _____ with friends in the library. Then they _____ dinner together.	4. _____ with friends. Then we _____ together.
Italian food is her favorite. She…	_____ food is my favorite. I…
5. _____ a good place for pizza and pasta.	5. _____ a good place for _____.
6. (not) _____ there often. It's expensive.	6. (not) _____ there often.

C 🔁 Now complete the information above about yourself. Tell a partner.

6 COMMUNICATION

A You are having a dinner party. Read about your six dinner guests.

Mary

She's from London, England. She plays guitar in a band. She doesn't eat meat. She is Danny's girlfriend.

Lisa

She's from Manila, in the Philippines. She's an actress. She speaks English, Spanish, and Tagalog. She doesn't drink alcohol.

Paula

She's from São Paulo, Brazil. She studies art at the University of London. She likes soccer.

Tomas

He's from the Dominican Republic. He speaks English and Spanish. He loves spicy food. He plays baseball.

Danny

He's from Los Angeles, in the United States. He's an actor. His brother works in South America. He loves Italian food.

Diego

He's from Buenos Aires, Argentina. He lives in Canada now. He teaches music at the University of Toronto.

B  Plan the party!

1. With a partner, make a menu for the dinner party.

   Think about your dinner guests' likes and dislikes.

2. Choose a seat at the table for each person. Include yourself and your partner.

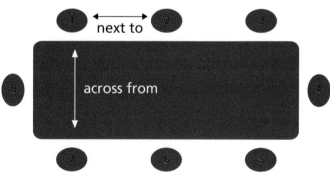

C Get together with a new pair. Explain your menu and table seating.

> Here's our menu. For dinner, we are having....

> Paula is in seat one. She's next to Tomas. They both like sports. She's across from....

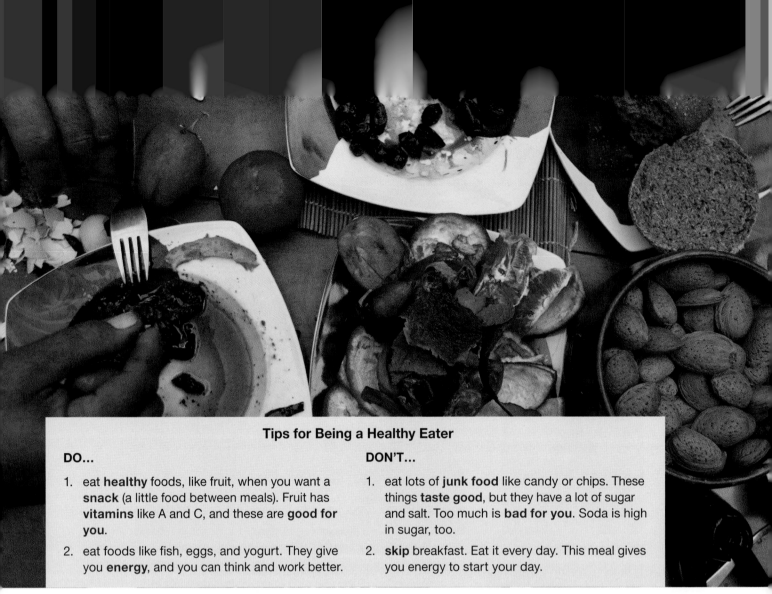

Tips for Being a Healthy Eater

DO...

1. eat **healthy** foods, like fruit, when you want a **snack** (a little food between meals). Fruit has **vitamins** like A and C, and these are **good for you**.

2. eat foods like fish, eggs, and yogurt. They give you **energy**, and you can think and work better.

DON'T...

1. eat lots of **junk food** like candy or chips. These things **taste good**, but they have a lot of sugar and salt. Too much is **bad for you**. Soda is high in sugar, too.

2. **skip** breakfast. Eat it every day. This meal gives you energy to start your day.

1 VOCABULARY

A 🔁 Read the tips above. Then answer the questions.

1. To be a healthy eater, what is good to do? What's not good to do? Why?

2. Which tips do you do? Tell a partner.

> I don't eat junk food. I don't like it.

Word Bank
Opposites
good for you ↔ bad for you
healthy ↔ unhealthy
have / eat breakfast ↔ skip breakfast
taste good ↔ taste bad

B 🔳 Complete the sentences with a partner. Use new ideas. Then tell another pair.

To be healthy:

1. eat foods high / low in....

2. don't eat.... It tastes good, but it's bad for you.

3. only drink a little.... Too much is bad for you.

4. don't skip....

5. eat.... It gives you energy.

6. eat...for a snack.

C 🔁 Make a poster with a partner using your ideas from **B**. Share your poster with the class and vote for a winner.

2 LISTENING

A 🔊 **Make and check predictions.** The items in the photos are used to make a smoothie. Guess: What is a smoothie? Circle your answer. Then listen to check your answer. **Track 4**

a. a soup   b. a drink   c. a main dish   d. a dessert

milk   ice   bananas   honey   ice cream

strawberries   oranges   yogurt

B 🔊 **Listen for details.** Listen again. What is <u>not</u> used to make the smoothie? Put an X on it. **Track 4**

C 🔊 **Listen for sequence.** How do you make the smoothie? Put the pictures in order from 1 to 7. Then listen and check your answers. **Track 5**

cut it into pieces

blend everything

peel the fruit

add the other ingredients

put oranges in the blender

put ice in the blender

add the other fruit

D 🔄 Tell a partner how to make a smoothie. Use your answers in **C**.

> To make a smoothie, first you.... Then you....

E 🔄 Do you ever drink smoothies? Are they healthy? What's in them? Tell a partner.

3 READING 🔊 Track 6

A 🔁 Find the words in *italics* below in your dictionary. Then answer the questions with a partner.

1. Which *illness—cancer* or a *cold—* is very bad?

2. Where is your *stomach*? Where is your *skin*? Point to each one.

B 🔁 **Scan for information.** Read and answer questions 1–3 about your food only.

Student A: Read about chili peppers.

Student B: Read about licorice.

1. Where does the food come from?
2. How do people use it today?
3. Why is it good for us?

C 🔁 Ask your partner the questions in **B** about his or her food. What are the answers? Take notes.

D **Read for details.** Are statements 1–9 about chilies (C), licorice (L), or both (B)? Write the correct letter.

_____ 1. is / are high in vitamin C

_____ 2. is / are in cold medicine

_____ 3. give(s) you energy

_____ 4. come(s) from Asia and Europe

_____ 5. can help people with cancer

_____ 6. is / are in sweet foods and drinks

_____ 7. make(s) you less hungry

_____ 8. come(s) from the Americas

_____ 9. can stop stomach and skin problems

E 🔁 Name another healthy food. Answer the questions in **B** about it. Tell a partner.

TWO POWERFUL HEALTH FOODS

Chili peppers are a type of fruit from the Americas. They were first used 6,000 years ago! Today, people all over the world, from Mexico to Thailand, use chilies in their cooking.

Chili peppers taste good, but they're also good for us. They are high in[1] vitamin C. This keeps you healthy. Many chilies are also spicy. This spice gives you energy. It also makes you less hungry, so you eat less. Doctors think chili peppers can stop some kinds of cancer, too.

[1] If something is *high in* vitamin C, it has a lot of vitamin C.

Red chili peppers

Licorice, a type of plant, comes from southern Europe and Asia. Today, when people hear the word *licorice*, they think of candy. In fact, licorice is in some sweet foods (like candy) and drinks (like soda), but it is also a very old medicine.[2] Two thousand years ago, people used licorice for colds and other illnesses. Today, it is still in some cold medicines. People also use it for stomach and skin problems. And now doctors think licorice—like chili peppers—can help people with cancer!

[2] *Medicine* is something you drink or eat to stop an illness.

Red licorice candy has no real licorice in it. Black licorice is much healthier!

4 GRAMMAR

A Turn to page 70. Complete the exercises. Then do **B–D** below.

Simple Present *Yes / No* Questions				Short Answers
Do	you	like	spicy food?	Yes, I do. / No, I don't.
	they			Yes, they do. / No, they don't.
Does	he / she			Yes, he / she does. / No, he / she doesn't.

B Read the sentences. Add one more sentence about eating and health.

Find someone who...	Classmate's name
1. has breakfast every day.	
2. drinks two glasses of water every day.	
3. eats a lot of junk food.	
4. drinks soda every day.	
5. likes spicy food.	
6. takes vitamins.	
7. eats a healthy snack every day.	
8. _____ .	

C 👥 Use the sentences in **B** to ask your classmates *Yes / No* questions. Find a different person for each answer. Write the person's name. The winner is the person to complete the chart first!

D 🔄 Tell a partner about three answers from your chart in **B**.

> Do you have breakfast every day?

> No, I don't. But I drink three sodas every day.

> That's a lot!

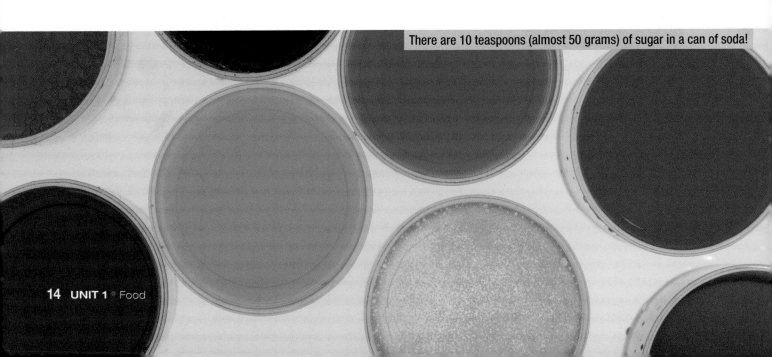

There are 10 teaspoons (almost 50 grams) of sugar in a can of soda!

5 WRITING

A Answer the questions about your favorite food. Write your ideas in a few words.

1. What is your favorite food?

2. Where is it from?

3. What's in it?

4. When do people eat it (for breakfast, lunch, dinner, or as a snack)?

5. Is it good or bad for you? Why?

B Use your notes in **A** to write a paragraph about your food. Use the example to help you.

My favorite dish is paella. It is from Spain. People eat it for lunch. It has rice, chicken, seafood, onions, tomatoes, vegetables, and a spice called saffron. It's delicious and very healthy. It's high in protein, and the vegetables are good for you, too.

6 COMMUNICATION

A Prepare a short talk about your favorite food.

1. Practice: Use your notes from Writing **A** to talk about your food. Do not just read your paragraph.

2. Find a photo, a map, or a video clip to use in your presentation.

B 👥 Work in a group of four. Give your presentation. Then listen to the other members of your group. When you listen, take notes. Answer the questions in Writing **A** about your partners' foods.

C 👥 Your group talked about four foods. Do you like each one? Why or why not? Take turns asking and telling the group.

Do you like pizza?

It's okay, but it's not very healthy. Do you like it?

Yeah, I love it!

TIME

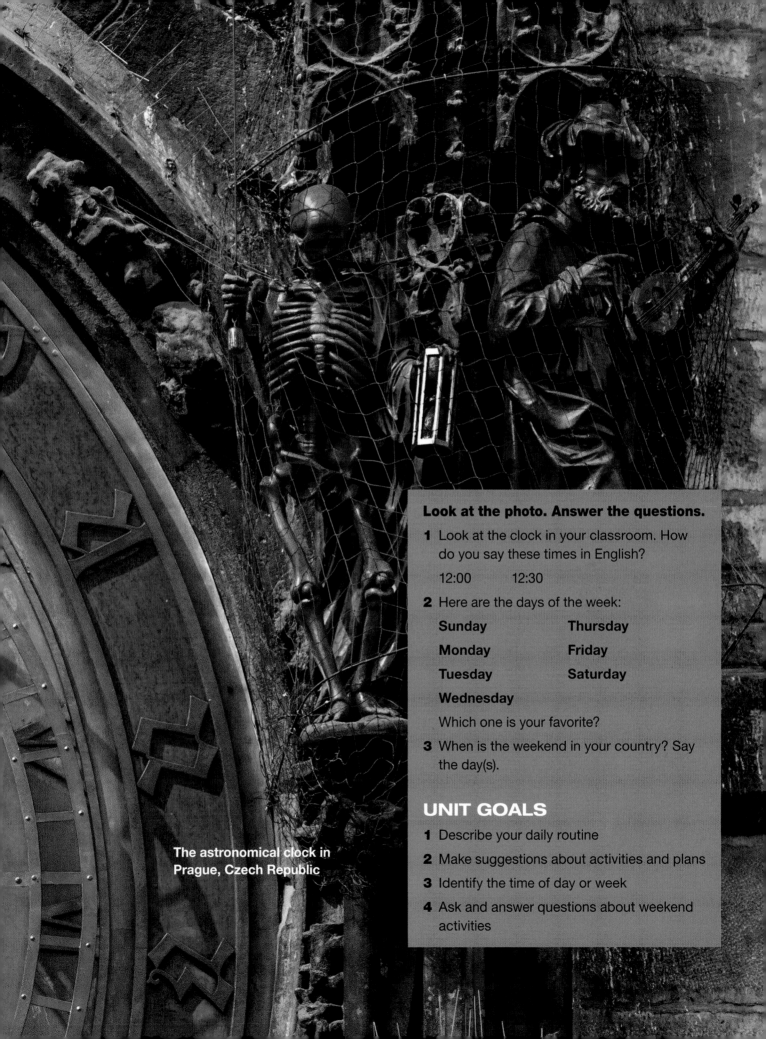

The astronomical clock in Prague, Czech Republic

Look at the photo. Answer the questions.

1 Look at the clock in your classroom. How do you say these times in English?

12:00   12:30

2 Here are the days of the week:

Sunday	**Thursday**
Monday	**Friday**
Tuesday	**Saturday**
Wednesday	

Which one is your favorite?

3 When is the weekend in your country? Say the day(s).

UNIT GOALS

1 Describe your daily routine

2 Make suggestions about activities and plans

3 Identify the time of day or week

4 Ask and answer questions about weekend activities

People rush through a busy train station in Germany.

1 VIDEO Late for Work

A Before you watch, do this:

1. Look up the word *late* in your dictionary.
2. Look at the pictures and the vocabulary on page 19.

B ▶ The man in the video starts work at 9:00. Watch the first 30 seconds. Circle your answer.

The man is / isn't late for work.

C ▶ Watch the entire video. What does the man do in the video? Put the events in order from 1 to 7.

_____ He washes his face.   _____ He reads a text message.   _____ He gets dressed.

_____ He wakes up.   _____ He has breakfast.   _____ He leaves home.

_____ He brushes his teeth.

D 🔄 Answer the questions with a partner.

1. Look at the sentence in **B** again. Is the man late for work? How do you know?
2. Does this ever happen to you?

2 VOCABULARY

A Study the times below. Then cover up the words and take turns telling the time with a partner.

What time is it?

It's....

five after four;
four-oh-five

nine fifteen;
quarter after nine

eleven forty-five;
quarter to twelve

two (o'clock)

eight thirty;
half past eight

two fifty-five;
five to three

B Practice telling the times shown below with a partner. Then read about Hiro's daily routine.

He wakes up at 7:30
and has breakfast.

Then he takes a shower
and gets dressed.

8:20

He leaves home at 8:20
and goes to school.

9:00

His classes start at 9:00 and
finish at 4:00.

4:50

At 4:50, he studies English.

5:45

After that, he goes home
at 5:45.

12:00

He eats dinner at 8:00. He
goes to bed at midnight.

C Use the words in **B** to tell your partner about your daily routine.

I wake up at 5:30.

That's early!

Word Bank

early = before the usual time

3 LISTENING

A [icon] Look at the words *yesterday*, *today*, and *tomorrow* in the box. Then complete the sentences. Compare answers with a partner.

If today is Friday, then tomorrow is _____. Yesterday was _____.

> ☀ ☾
>
> **Yesterday** ⬅ **Today / Tonight** ➡ **Tomorrow**
> Monday   Tuesday   Wednesday

B [icon] **Listen for gist.** Pilar and Alma are talking about Pilar's plans for today and tomorrow. Write *today* or *tomorrow* for each activity. **Track 7**

1. go to school _____
2. have a piano lesson _____
3. see a movie _____
4. study English _____
5. take a swimming class _____
6. take a test _____

C [icon] **Listen for details.** Write your *today* answers from **B** on lines 1–4 below. When does Pilar plan to do each of these activities? Listen again and write the start and finish times. **Track 7**

Activity	Start Time	Finish Time
1. _____	_____	_____
2. _____	_____	_____
3. _____	_____	_____
4. _____	_____	_____

D [icon] Tell a partner about Pilar's day.

> Pilar goes to school at....

E [icon] **Pronunciation: Numbers.** Listen and repeat. Notice the different stress. **Track 8**

13 / 30   14 / 40   15 / 50   16 / 60   17 / 70   18 / 80   19 / 90

F [icon] **Pronunciation: Numbers.** Listen to the sentences. Circle the correct answer. **Track 9**

1. I wake up at 6:14 / 6:40 every morning.
2. The train to school takes about 19 / 90 minutes.
3. She drives 17 / 70 kilometers to work.
4. After dinner, I study for an hour and 15 / 50 minutes.
5. It's his birthday today. He's 16 / 60 years old.

G [icon] [icon] **Pronunciation: Numbers.** Listen again and check your answers. Take turns saying the sentences in **F** with a partner. **Track 9**

4 SPEAKING

A 🔊 ⊘ Listen to the conversation. Then complete the sentences with a partner. Circle the correct answer. **Track 10**

1. Adriano   Jessie   Both   ...want(s) to eat French food tonight.
2. Adriano   Jessie   Both   ...want(s) to see the new superhero movie.
3. Adriano   Jessie   Both   ...want(s) to see the James Bond movie.

It's noon.

It's midnight.

ADRIANO: What do you want to do tonight, Jessie?

JESSIE: I don't know. Hey, let's have dinner at that new French restaurant.

ADRIANO: Hmmm... I don't really like French food. And I'm not very hungry.

JESSIE: OK, well, we could see a movie.

ADRIANO: Yeah, that sounds good. Let's see the new superhero movie.

JESSIE: Hmmm... I don't really want to see that. What else is playing?

ADRIANO: Well, the new James Bond movie is at the AMC Theater.

JESSIE: Great idea. When is it playing?

ADRIANO: At 8:15.

JESSIE: At 8:50?

ADRIANO: No, *8:15*. And there's a late show at midnight.

JESSIE: Midnight is late! Let's go to the 8:15 show.

ADRIANO: OK!

B ⊘ Practice the conversation with a partner.

SPEAKING STRATEGY

C ⊘ Use the Useful Expressions to complete the dialogs. Then practice with a partner.

1. A: What do you want for lunch?

   B: _____ Mexican food.

   A: _____. I love Mexican food!

2. A: What do you want to do after class?

   B: _____ play video games.

   A: _____ video games.

   B: OK, well, _____ see a movie.

   A: _____. What do you want to see?

Useful Expressions
Making suggestions
Making a suggestion
Let's see a movie.
We could see a movie.
Saying *yes*
(That) sounds good.
Good / Great idea.
Saying *no* politely
I don't really like French food.
I don't really want to see that movie.

D ⊘ Add three or four more lines to dialog 2 in **C**.

Student B: Suggest a movie to see.

Student A: You don't want to see Student B's movie. Suggest another idea.

Students A & B: Agree on a movie and a time to see it.

5 GRAMMAR

A Turn to page 71. Complete the exercises. Then do **B–D** below.

	Prepositions of Time
When is your class?	It's **on** Monday(s). / It's **on** Tuesday night.
	It's **in** the morning / afternoon / evening. It's **at** night.
	It's **at** 8:30 / noon.
	It's **from** 4:00 **to** 5:30. / It's **from** Tuesday **to** Saturday.

B Complete the answer choices with *in*, *at*, *on*, *from*, or *to*. Then choose the answers that are true for you.

1. When do you like to study?
   a. _____ the morning
   b. _____ the afternoon
   c. _____ the evening
   d. late _____ night

2. When do you do most of your homework?
   a. _____ weekdays
   b. _____ Saturdays and Sundays
   c. both

3. What day is your birthday this year?
   a. It's _____ Monday.
   b. It's _____ Tuesday.
   c. It's _____ Wednesday.
   d. other: _____

4. You can see a movie with your friends _____ noon or _____ midnight.
   Which do you choose? _____

5. What is your favorite subject at school? What time does the class meet?
   My favorite subject is _____.
   The class is _____ _____ from _____ _____ _____.
                (day(s) of the week)   (start time)   (end time)

People study at the library at Colegio de San Nicolas in San Michoacan, Mexico.

C Now interview a partner. Use the questions in **B**. Take notes.

D What is one new thing you know about your partner now? Tell him or her.

> You do your homework on weekdays and Saturdays and Sundays. I think you're a serious student.

6 COMMUNICATION

A Read the directions below.

1. At the top of the schedule, write today's day (Monday, Tuesday, etc.) and the next two days.

2. Complete the calendar with your schedule for these three days (school, work, English or music lessons, an appointment, seeing friends, etc.). You can also add new ideas. Write the activities next to the times in the calendar. If you have no plans, leave the time blank.

9:00 AM			
10:00 AM			
11:00 AM			
NOON			
1:00 PM			
2:00 PM			
3:00 PM			
4:00 PM			
5:00 PM			
6:00 PM			
7:00 PM			

B Work with a partner. Read the example. Then find time in both your schedules to do the three activities together.

- practice English   • see a movie   • your idea: _____

    A: Let's study together for the test. Are you free today at 1:00?

    B: No, sorry, I'm busy. Are you free tomorrow?

    A: Well, I have classes from 11:00 to 4:00, but then I'm free.

    B: OK, let's meet at 4:15.

    A: That sounds good!

People at a party in Amsterdam.

1 VOCABULARY

A  Look at the photo. Where are these people? Do you ever do this on the weekend with your friends? Tell a partner.

B Look at the activities with *go* in the Word Bank and read sentences 1–4. Then complete 5–10.

On the weekend, I usually...

1. _go for a walk_. (a walk)
2. _go dancing_. (dance)
3. _go to a party_. (a party)
4. _go out with friends_. (with friends)
5. _____. (the movies)
6. _____. (a bike ride)
7. _____. (shop)
8. _____. (a friend's house)
9. _____. (with my family)
10. _____. (the gym)

Word Bank
Activities with *go*
go + *-ing* verb
go dancing
go to + a place
go to a party / the beach
go for + an activity
go for a walk
go out + *with* + someone
go out with friends

C In **B**, check (✓) the activities you do on the weekend.

D  Compare your answers with a partner's. Are your weekends similar or different? Do you do other activities?

2 LISTENING

A 🔄 Read the sentences. Then tell a partner: Is a *day off* a free day or a workday?

Tomorrow is my <u>day off</u>. I don't work or go to school.

B 🔊 **Listen for details.** Nick and Kelly are talking. Listen. Check (✓) the days Nick works. Put an *X* on his day(s) off. **Track 11**

☐ Monday

☐ Friday

☐ Saturday

☐ Sunday

C 🔊 **Listen for details.** What is good and bad about Nick's day(s) off? Listen. Write one word in each blank. **Track 12**

Good: Most people are at work or _____. Most places aren't _____.

Bad: Nick's friends are _____. He does most things _____.

D 🔊 **Listen for details.** Listen again. Check (✓) the things Nick does on his day off. **Track 12**

☐ He goes shopping.   ☐ He goes for a bike ride.

☐ He goes to the movies.   ☐ He wakes up late.

☐ He does homework.   ☐ He goes out with friends.

E 🔄 Is your day off similar to or different from Nick's? Why? Tell a partner.

3 READING Track 13

A Look at the pictures in the reading. What are the people doing? Tell a partner.

B **Make predictions.** Match a person (1, 2, 3, or 4) with one or more activities (a–f) below.

Person

1. The Couch Potato ___________
2. The Workaholic ___________
3. The Party Animal ___________
4. The Health Nut ___________

Activity

a. likes to exercise
b. wakes up late on the weekend
c. goes out all night
d. doesn't like to go out on weekends
e. is always thinking about work or school
f. wakes up early

C **Check predictions; Read for specific information.** Now read the article. Check your answers in **B**.

D Work in a group of 3–4 people. Answer the questions.

1. What kind of weekend person are you? Why? Which type is most common in your group?
2. Think of something you want to do this weekend. Suggest it to your partners. Can you all agree?
3. What kind of weekend person is your best friend?

THE HEALTH NUT

For you, the weekend isn't a time to relax; you want to go out and do things! You usually wake up early (yes, even on the weekend) and go for a walk, a run, or a bike ride. All week, you're inside at school or work. On the weekend, it's time to go outside and be active!

WHAT KIND
OF WEEKEND PERSON
ARE YOU?

For many people, the weekend is a time to relax and have fun. But not everyone has fun in the same way. Here's how different people spend their weekends. What type of person are you?

THE COUCH POTATO

What's your perfect weekend? Sleeping late, watching TV, and playing video games. Sure, you like to spend time with[1] friends—but only at home.

[1] If you *spend time with* people, you do something together.

THE WORKAHOLIC

It's the weekend and it's time to relax… but not for you. The Workaholic is always busy: working, studying, talking on the phone, texting classmates, or checking emails. When you go out with friends on the weekend, you're thinking about your homework or your next exam.

THE PARTY ANIMAL

For you, the weekend is all about fun—and lots of it. Your night starts at 9:00 or 10:00. You go dancing or to a party with friends. Later, you go home and sleep all day. Then you wake up in the afternoon and do it all again!

4 GRAMMAR

A Turn to pages 71–72. Complete the exercises. Then do **B** and **C** below.

Simple Present *Wh-* Questions				
Question word	***do / does***	**Subject**	**Verb**	**Answers**
Who	do	you	study with?	(I study with) Maria.
What	does	she	do on Saturdays?	(She) goes out with friends.
When	do	they	have class?	(They have class) at 9:00.
		we		(We have class) on Mondays.
Where	does	he		(He has class) in Room 3B.

B 🔁 Read about Zoe's weekend. Unscramble questions 1–4. Start each sentence with a question word. Then ask and answer the questions with a partner.

On Saturday, Zoe...	On Sunday, Zoe...
• works at a department store from 9:00 AM to 3:30 PM. • goes to the gym in the afternoon. • goes out with friends at night.	• wakes up at 11:00 AM. • goes for a bike ride in the afternoon. • studies in the evening.

1. Zoe / what / do / on Saturday afternoon / does

   _____? *She goes to the gym* _____.

2. she / work / does / when

   _____? _____.

3. does / work / she / where

   _____? _____.

4. who / on Saturday night / Zoe / does / go out with

   _____? _____.

C 🔁 Write four more questions about Zoe's schedule. Use different question words. Then ask and answer the questions with a partner.

1. _____
2. _____
3. _____
4. _____

> What time does Zoe get up on Sunday?

5 WRITING

A Read the texts between Raquel and her friends, Monika and Alex. Answer the questions with a partner.

1. What does Raquel suggest?
2. Who says *yes*? What does the person suggest?
3. What do these symbols mean in the texts?

Raquel
Hey guys, let's go dancing tonight at Club Skye.

Alex
OK. Let's meet there @ 10 PM

Monika
I can't. I have homework.

Raquel
Monika
Alex

B Write a text to a partner. Suggest something to do tonight or this weekend. Say when and where it is.

C Exchange texts with your partner. Read his or her message. Then write a text back saying *yes* or *no*. If you say *no*, give a reason.

D Repeat **B** and **C** with a new partner.

6 COMMUNICATION

A Read the questions on the left side of the chart. In the *Me* column, check (✓) the activities you do.

Do you...	Me	Classmates	Question	Details
watch TV?			What... ?	
go shopping?			Where... ?	
wake up late?			When... ?	
go out with friends?			Where... ?	
do homework?			What... ?	
spend time with family?			Who... ?	
your idea: _____			_____	

B Interview your classmates. For each question, find a different person to answer *yes*. Write the classmate's name. Ask another question to get more details.

Do you watch TV on the weekend?

Yes, I do.

What do you watch?

On Sunday night, I watch....

C Read your notes. What is the most interesting answer? Tell the class.

3 SPECIAL OCCASIONS

Three young women are dressed up for Day of the Dead in Mexico.

Look at the photo. Answer the questions.

1 Where is this festival and when does it happen?

2 Special occasions happen in different seasons. The seasons are:

   winter   spring   summer   fall
   Which season is your favorite?

3 Here are some more seasons. Which ones happen where you live?
   rainy season   dry season
   hurricane / typhoon season

UNIT GOALS

1 Talk about important dates

2 Express degrees of certainty

3 Describe when special occasions happen and how they are celebrated

4 Describe what happens at a festival

LESSON A HOLIDAYS

Instruments at the Ice Music Festival

1 VIDEO Ice Music

A Look at the photo above. This video is about "ice music." What do you think ice music is?

B ▶ Watch the video. Circle the correct answer(s).

1. This happens in Norway / Iceland.

2. They make / play ice instruments.

3. They make / cut the ice.

C 🔁 Do you like this music? Tell a partner.

D 🔁 With a partner, plan a music festival. Write down where it takes place, what instruments there are, and who goes. Share your ideas with the class.

2 VOCABULARY

A Practice saying the months of the year with a partner.

January	
February	
March	
April	
May	
June	
July	
August	
September	
October	
November	
December	

B Work with a partner.

- Name as many holidays as you can.
- Write each one next to the correct month.
- In two minutes, try to fill up the chart.

C Tell another pair about your list. Which holiday is your favorite?

> In our list, we have Loy Krathong for November.

Loy Krathong Festival, Thailand

3 LISTENING

A 🔊 🔁 **Pronunciation: *th* and *t*.** Practice saying these ordinal numbers with a partner. Then listen and repeat. **Track 14**

1st first	6th sixth	11th eleventh	30th thirtieth
2nd second	7th seventh	12th twelfth	40th fortieth
3rd third	8th eighth	13th thirteenth	50th fiftieth
4th fourth	9th ninth	↓	↓
5th fifth	10th tenth	20th twentieth	100th one hundredth

B 🔁 A student is flying home for summer vacation. Look at the plane ticket below. Then answer the questions with a partner.

1. Where is the person going?

2. How much is the ticket?

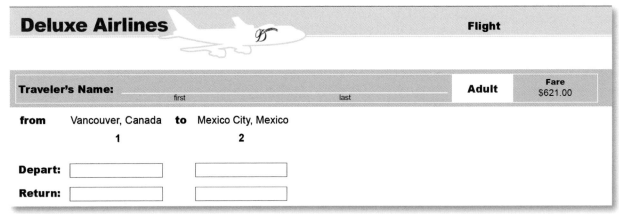

Deluxe Airlines 𝒟   **Flight**

Traveler's Name:		**Adult**	**Fare** $621.00
first	last		

from Vancouver, Canada **to** Mexico City, Mexico
             1   **2**

Depart: [＿＿＿＿] [＿＿＿＿]
Return: [＿＿＿＿] [＿＿＿＿]

C 🔊 **Listen for numbers and dates.** Listen and complete the information on the ticket with the man's name. What day is he departing? What day is he returning? Write your answers under *1*. **Track 15**

D 🔊 **Listen for numbers and dates.** The man changes his travel dates. Listen and write the new dates under *2*. Cross out the old fare and write the new one. **Track 16**

E 🔁 Look at the travel dates in **D**. Answer these questions with a partner.

1. Are these good dates to travel in your country?

2. What are the best months for traveling in your country?

Vancouver, Canada

4 SPEAKING

A 🔊 Kendrick and Tanya are studying in the United States. Listen to their conversation. Then answer the questions. **Track 17**

1. What holiday is on the first Monday in September in the United States?

2. What do people do on this day? Does Tanya know?

TANYA: So, Kendrick... do you have plans for Labor Day?

KENDRICK: Labor Day?

TANYA: Yeah, it's a holiday here in the US. We have the day off from school.

KENDRICK: Really? When is it?

TANYA: It's on the first Monday in September.

KENDRICK: Sounds good. So, do people do anything special?

TANYA: I'm not sure. It's a long weekend, so some people travel. My host family plans to have a barbecue.

B 🔁 Practice the conversation in **A** with a partner.

SPEAKING STRATEGY

C 🔁 Answer the questions with a partner. Use the Useful Expressions to help you.

Useful Expressions		
Saying you know or don't know something		
Is tomorrow a holiday?		When is Labor Day?
Yes, it is. / No, it isn't.	certain	It's on September 3rd this year.
I'm not sure. It could be.	not sure	I'm not sure. Is it in September?
I don't (really) know.	don't know	I don't (really) know.

Speaking Tip

Follow-up questions:

I'm not sure. Is it in September?

I don't know. What do you think?

1. When is Mexico's Independence Day?

   a. May 5th

   b. August 24th

   c. September 16th

2. Where is the New Year called *Hogmanay*?

   a. in Russia

   b. in Scotland

   c. in Iceland

3. Where does Children's Day happen on May 5th?

   a. in Italy and Greece

   b. in Chile and Peru

   c. in Korea and Japan

4. What holiday is on October 31st in the United States?

   a. Halloween

   b. Thanksgiving

   c. Christmas

> Where is the New Year called *Hogmanay*?

> I don't really know. What do you think?

D 🔺 Check your answers on page 79. Who has the most correct answers in your class?

5 GRAMMAR

A Turn to page 72. Complete the exercise. Then do **B–D** below.

Prepositions of Time: *in* and *on*	
When is the holiday party?	It's **on** December 20th. / It's **on** Christmas Eve. / It's **on** Monday.
	It's **in** December. / It's **in** the winter. / It's **in** (early / late) 2016.

B 🔁 Study the grammar chart. Then follow
the steps below.

1. **Student A:** Read the items in Group 1 aloud to
   Student B. Write the answers Student B gives.

2. **Student B:** Close your book and listen to your
   partner. Say the correct preposition for each item.
   Answer as quickly as you can.

3. Switch roles and repeat with the items in Group 2.

spring   summer   fall / autumn winter

Group 1	Group 2
1. _____ 2002	1. _____ May
2. _____ the third Tuesday of the month	2. _____ December 31st
3. _____ March	3. _____ the first Saturday of the month
4. _____ New Year's Day	4. _____ the nineties
5. _____ the spring	5. _____ 2004
6. _____ January 1st	6. _____ the summer
7. _____ the eighties	7. _____ Labor Day

> OK, let's start.
> Number one.
> 2002.

> **In** 2002!

C Complete as much information as you can about your own birthdate.

Your special day		
1. date (e.g., the 17th)		1. _____
2. month		2. _____
3. year		3. _____
4. decade	of your birth	4. _____
5. season		5. _____
6. day of the week		6. _____
7. time of day*		7. _____

> ℹ️ A *decade*
> is a period
> of ten years. For
> the decade of the
> 1990s you can say
> *(in) the nineteen
> nineties* or just *(in)
> the nineties.*

*morning, afternoon, or evening

D 🔁 Interview a partner about his or her
birthdate. Are you similar in any way?

> What is the month of your
> birth?

> I was born in November.

6 COMMUNICATION

A 🔗 On some holidays or special days, there are expressions people say. Look at the examples in the box. Then do the following:

- What holidays, or special days, are in the photos below? Tell a partner.

- Match an expression in the box with a photo. Write the letter of the expression on the photo.

- Take turns with a partner saying the expression in English for each holiday or special day.

- In your country, what do people say on these days? Tell your partner.

a. Happy Birthday!
b. Congratulations!
c. Happy New Year!
d. Happy Mother's Day.
e. I love you. / Happy Valentine's Day.

On New Year's Day, people in my country say....

B Answer the questions.

1. What is your favorite day of the year? _____

2. When is it? _____

3. What do you eat or drink on this day? _____

4. What do you do or where do you go? _____

C 🔲 Get into a group of four. Share your answers from **B**. Which day of the year is the most popular?

The Highland Games take place **annually** (every year) in the spring and fall all over Scotland.

*What happens at the **festival**:*

- People wear **traditional** clothes and play traditional sports. One popular **event** is the hammer throw.
- There are bagpipe **parades**.
- People from around the world **perform** traditional Scottish dances. They **compete** to be the best.
- Thousands of people **attend** the games. People also **celebrate** the games in countries like Brazil and New Zealand.
- Don't **miss** the festival, and **take** lots of **photos**!

Women do a traditional Scottish dance.

A man competes in the hammer throwing event.

1 VOCABULARY

Word Bank
Saying how often something happens
daily, weekly, monthly, annually every two / three / four years

A 🔁 Read about the Highland Games. Look up any words you don't know. Then ask and answer the questions with a partner.

1. Where are the games? _____

2. How often do they take place? _____

3. When do they take place? _____

4. How many people attend? _____

5. What happens at the games? _____

6. Is this event interesting to you? Why? _____

B 🔁 Think of another sporting event or sports festival. Answer questions 1–6 in **A** about it. Tell a partner about the event or festival.

People at Oktoberfest in Munich

2 LISTENING

A 🔄 **Infer information.** Look at the photo. Then answer the questions with a partner.

1. Do you know anything about this festival?

2. Guess: What kind of festival is it?

B 🔊 **Listen for details.** Read the sentences. Then listen. Circle the correct words. **Track 18**

1. Both festivals are spring / summer / winter / autumn festivals.

2. Oktoberfest is a(n) art / food / film / music festival.

3. The Moon Festival is an important art / family / film / sports event.

C 🔊 **Listen for details.** Read the sentences. Then listen again. Write one word or number in each blank. **Track 18**

	Oktoberfest	The Moon Festival
Where does it take place?	in Munich, _____	in _____
When is it?	for _____ days in late _____ or early _____	in late _____ or early _____
What do people do?	eat _____ German food	spend time with _____, eat moon _____, and _____ with colorful lanterns
What other countries have this festival?	_____ and _____	Vietnam and Singapore

D 🔄 Choose one festival. Tell your partner about it. Use your notes.

> The Moon Festival takes place in....

E 🔄 Are there autumn festivals in your country? Are they similar to Oktoberfest or the Moon Festival? Tell a partner.

3 READING 🔊 Track 19

A 🔁 **Infer information.** Look at the photo on the next page with a partner. Guess: Where are the people? What kind of festival is Burning Man?

B 🔁 **Scan for information.** Look quickly at the article. Find answers to the questions. Then ask and answer the questions with a partner.

1. How many people attend Burning Man? _____

2. Where does it take place? _____

3. When is it? _____

4. How long is it? _____

5. What type of festival is it? _____

6. What happens at the end? _____

C **Read for details.** Read the passage closely. Check (✓) the things you can do at Burning Man. Put an X next to the things you cannot do.

_____ play music related to the theme

_____ share things

_____ ride a bicycle

_____ sell clothes

_____ buy food

_____ see interesting art

D 🔁 **Exemplify.** Sit back-to-back with a partner. Imagine you are at Burning Man. Call your partner on the phone. Talk about the festival: What do you see? What are you doing? Is it fun?

E 🔁 Do you think Burning Man is an interesting festival? Why or why not? Is there a similar festival in your country? Tell a partner.

BURNING MAN

Every year, over 60,000 people from all over the world attend the Burning Man festival in the Black Rock Desert in the US. The eight-day event starts on the last Monday in August and ends on the first Monday in September, which is Labor Day in the US.

Every year, Burning Man has a different theme. Some past themes are Time, Good and Bad, The Body, and Hope and Fear. People make art, play music, and wear clothes related to the theme. There are also many activities for people to do—all related to the theme.

The Burning Man festival is very large—about one-and-a-half miles (almost 2.5 km). Many people use a bike to go from place to place. Also, festival-goers cannot buy anything at Burning Man, except some drinks (like water, coffee, and tea) and ice. For this reason, people bring their own food and drinks. They also share things with others.

On the last day, a large statue of a man is burned. It marks the end of summer and the Burning Man festival.

People watch the Burning Man statue burn at the end of the festival.

4 GRAMMAR

A Turn to pages 73–74. Complete the exercises. Then do **B–D** below.

When and How long Questions		
With be	**When** is the festival?	It's **in** July / **on** Thursday. It starts **on** July 1 / **at** 10:00.
	How long is the festival?	(It's) **from** July 1 **to** July 3. (It lasts) **until** July 3 / **for** three days.
With other verbs	**When** do you study?	(I study) **on** Saturdays / **in** the evening.
	How long do you study?	(I study) **from** 4:00 to 6:00 / **until** 6:00 / **for** an hour.

B 🔗 Complete the dialog with *When, How long,* or a preposition. Then practice in pairs.

A: _____ does your vacation start?

B: _____ Friday.

A: _____ is your break?

B: It lasts _____ two weeks, _____ July 3 _____ July 17.

A: So, do you have any plans?

B: Yeah. I'm going to Comic-Con in San Diego, California.

A: Cool! _____ do you leave?

B: _____ July 6.

A: _____ are you in the US?

B: I stay _____ July 13. I return home _____ the 14th.

A: Sounds good. So, _____ is the flight from Lima to San Diego?

B: Nine hours!

C 🔗 Think of a festival to go to. Make a new dialog with a partner.

D 🔗 Say your dialog for another pair. When you listen to the other pair, answer questions 1–4.

1. How long is the speaker's break?

2. Where is he or she going?

3. When does he or she leave?

4. How long does he or she stay at the festival?

Over 100,000 people attend Comic-Con International every year. At the event, you can learn about new comic books and science fiction movies and TV shows.

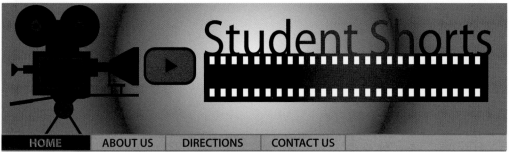

Student Shorts

| HOME | ABOUT US | DIRECTIONS | CONTACT US |

GUESTS:
Who's Attending

Emma Shea   Jose Alonso   Noah Kim

The 3rd Annual Student Shorts
Film Festival

Time:
Saturday and Sunday
May 8 & 9 | 6:00–11:00 PM

Location:
City College Student Union

More info:
Do you make YouTube videos? Enter your short video and you can win $1,000! Then come and see this year's best videos. Meet the student filmmakers and some famous YouTubers, too. Don't miss it!

This event is free for all students with ID.

5 WRITING

A Read the festival event page. Answer the questions with a partner.

1. What kind of festival is it?
2. What is the festival's name?
3. When and for how long is the festival?
4. Where does it take place?
5. What activities can you do at the festival?
6. Is the event free?

B Think of a festival with your partner. It can be a real one or you can create a new one. Answer questions 1–6 in **A** about it. Then create an event page for it like the one above.

C Give your event page to another pair. Read theirs. Answer the questions.

1. Does their event page answer questions 1–6 in **A**?
2. Are there any mistakes in the writing? If there are, correct them.
3. Can you make their event page better? Say one idea. Then return their page to them.

6 COMMUNICATION

A Get together with a new pair. Show them your event page and tell them about your festival. Repeat this step with five or six pairs in your class.

B Which festival is your favorite? Why? Complete the sentence below and tell the class. Which festivals are popular?

I plan to attend _____.

4 HOME

A stained glass house in Brooklyn, the United States

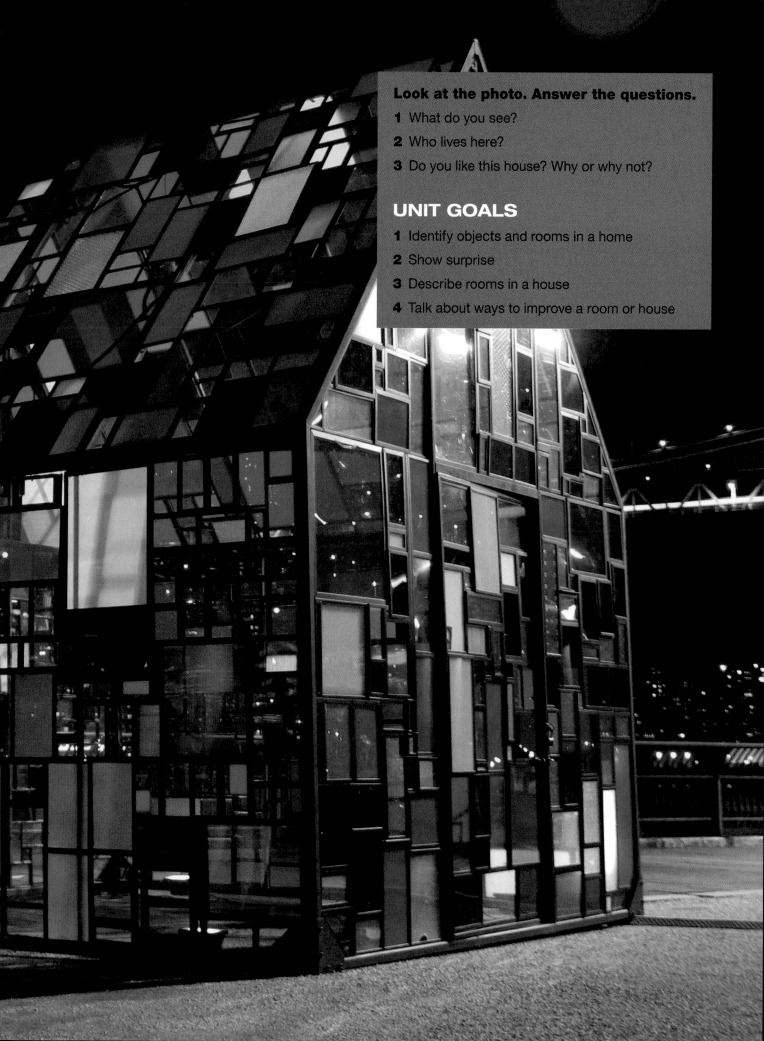

Look at the photo. Answer the questions.

1 What do you see?

2 Who lives here?

3 Do you like this house? Why or why not?

UNIT GOALS

1 Identify objects and rooms in a home

2 Show surprise

3 Describe rooms in a house

4 Talk about ways to improve a room or house

Many modern apartments have to use space in creative ways.

1 VIDEO Small Spaces, Small Ideas

A 🔄 Look at the photo. Is the room big or small? Is it a comfortable room? Do you like it? Tell a partner.

B ▶️ Watch the video with the sound off. You will see three rooms. Check the *two* things you see people doing in each room.

Room 1	Room 2	Room 3
☐ reading	☐ cooking	☐ studying
☐ playing	☐ watching TV	☐ watching TV
☐ cooking	☐ eating and drinking	☐ sleeping

C ▶️ Watch the video again. Is each room comfortable or not?

D 🔄 Explain your answers in **C** to a partner.

> I don't like room 2. It's very dark.

2 VOCABULARY

A Look at the apartment. With a partner, use the list to identify the different rooms, areas, and items.

ROOMS	AREAS
1. living room	6. balcony
2. dining room	7. elevator
3. kitchen	8. stairs
4. bedroom	9. yard
5. bathroom	10. garage

ITEMS		
a. sofa	f. wall	k. refrigerator
b. rug	g. window	l. stove
c. lamp	h. air conditioner	m. toilet
d. table	i. closet	n. sink
e. chair	j. bed	o. shower

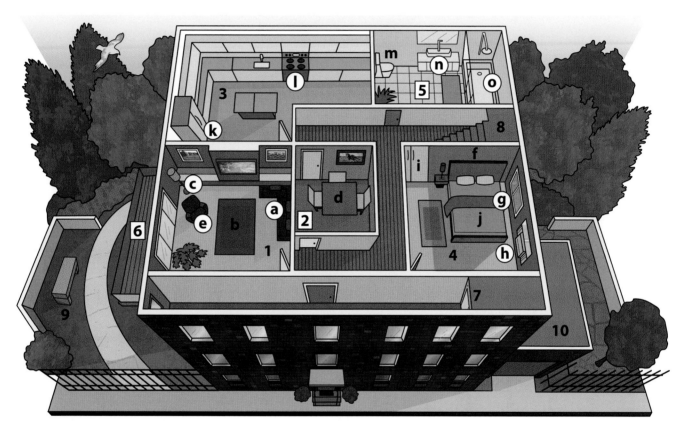

B Cover up the lists in **A**. Can you and your partner identify the different rooms, areas, and items?

C Ask and answer the questions with a partner.

1. What rooms are in your apartment or house?
2. Where are items *d*, *g*, and *i* in your home?
3. Where do you watch TV? cook? hang out with friends? sleep? eat dinner? take a shower?

> I usually hang out with my friends in the living room.

> My family cooks dinner in the kitchen.

3 LISTENING

A 🔊 ♻ **Pronunciation: Rising intonation to show surprise.** You can show surprise by repeating certain information with rising intonation (↗). Listen and repeat. Then practice the dialogs with a partner. **Track 20**

1. A: The rent is 2,000 a month.
   B: Two thousand? ↗ That's expensive!
2. A: There's no elevator in the building.
   B: No elevator? ↗ But you live on the sixth floor!
3. A: I live on a houseboat.
   B: A houseboat? ↗ That's cool!

B Look at the pictures in **D**. Name the rooms in each apartment.

C 🔊 **Listen for gist.** Yao is a student in Vancouver, Canada. He needs a place to live. Listen and check (✓) the correct answers. **Track 21**

CITY RENTALS

Name: *Yao Peng Wong* **Job:** *Student*

I want to rent...	☐ a house.	☐ an apartment.	☐ a room in a house.
I want to rent for...	☐ a month.	☐ nine months.	☐ twelve months.
I want to live...	☐ alone.	☐ with a roommate.	☐ with a family member.

D 🔊 **Listen for details.** Amy is telling Yao about three apartments. Listen and notice the rooms as Amy talks. Number the apartments 1–3. **Track 22**

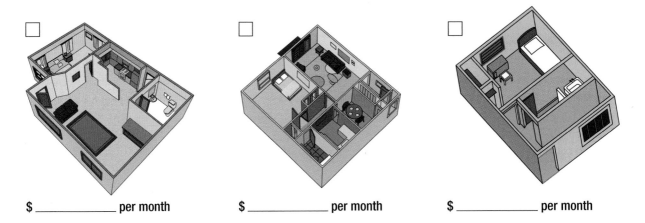

$ _____ per month $ _____ per month $ _____ per month

E 🔊 ♻ **Listen for numbers.** Listen again. Write the rent amount per month for each apartment in **D**. Circle the apartment Yao likes. What do you think of Yao's choice? Tell a partner. **Track 22**

4 SPEAKING

A 🔊 **Listen for a speaker's attitude.** In the conversation, Tim uses two expressions (underlined) to show surprise. Listen. Notice how Tim says these expressions. **Track 23**

TIM: Hey, Yao. How are you doing?

YAO: Hi, Tim. Come in.

TIM: Thanks. So, this is your new place. It's nice.

YAO: Yeah, and it's only $625 a month.

TIM: <u>Are you serious</u>? 625? That's cheap.

YAO: Yeah, *and* I've got free WiFi.

TIM: <u>No way</u>!

YAO: It's true. I've got a great apartment. There's just one problem.

TIM: What's that?

YAO: There's no elevator, and I'm on the sixth floor!

B 🔄 Practice the conversation with a partner.

SPEAKING STRATEGY

C 🔄 Make two new conversations with a partner. Use the Useful Expressions and the conversation above. Pay attention to your intonation (↗ or ↘).

Useful Expressions: Showing surprise	
Said with rising intonation ↗	Said with falling intonation ↘
My house has 20 rooms.	My house has 20 rooms.
Really?	You're kidding. / You're joking.
Are you serious?	No way. [informal]
For real? [informal]	(No,) it's true.
Yeah.	

Word Bank

I **live in** a house / an apartment building.

I **live on** the first / second / third / top floor.

D 👥 Read the examples below. Then tell four people something they don't know about you. If you cannot think of anything, make something up.

A: I play the guitar.

B: For real?

A: Yeah. I play in a band.

B: Where do you practice?

A: My sister lives near a famous soccer player.

B: You're kidding.

A: No, it's true.

B: What's his name?

E 👥 Which answer from **D** is the most interesting or unusual? Tell the class.

5 GRAMMAR

A Turn to pages 75–76. Complete the exercises. Then do **B–D** below.

There is / There are				
Singular	**There is** (There's) **There isn't**	a	rug	in my bedroom.
Plural	**There are** **There aren't** any		rugs	

Questions	Short answers
Is there an elevator in your building? **Are there** (any) windows in your living room?	Yes, **there is**. / No, **there isn't**. Yes, **there are**. / No, **there aren't** (any).
How many windows **are** (**there**) in your bedroom?	**There's** one. / **There are** two. / **There aren't** any.

B 🔄 Work with a partner. Look at the chart below. On a piece of paper, make as many sentences as you can.

There	are aren't is isn't	a any some two	chairs sofa TV windows	in the living room.

C Imagine your dream house. Answer the questions.

- How many rooms are there in your house? What are the rooms?
- What items are in each room?

D 🔄 Take turns asking and answering questions with a partner. Talk about your dream house.

> How many rooms are in your house?

> There are ten.

> Is there a bedroom?

> There are three bedrooms.

Adare Manor, Limerick, Ireland

6 COMMUNICATION

A Look at the picture and read about the bedroom.

In my room, the bed is **near** a big window. The window is **to the right** of the bed. Next to the bed (**on the right**), there's a small table with a lamp **on** it. There is also a table **to the left** of the bed. There is a mirror **above** my bed and a chair **in front of** my bed.

B 🔁 Talk about your room with a partner.

Student A: Think about your bedroom. On a piece of paper, draw your bedroom door and your bed. Then give the paper to your partner. What other things are in your room? Where are they? Tell your partner.

Student B: Listen to your partner's description. Draw your partner's bedroom.

Word Bank
mirror = a flat piece of glass that reflects things

C 🔁 **Student A:** Check your partner's drawing. Does it look like your room? Switch roles and do **B** again. Are your rooms similar or different?

The color fan labels: pink, orange, bright yellow, red, green, white, light blue, brown, blue, gray, dark blue, black, purple

1 VOCABULARY

A Say the colors with your instructor. Then ask a partner: What is your favorite color?

B Look at the photo. Answer the questions with a partner.

1. What things are in the room? What colors are they?

2. When you look at the room, how do you feel?

    Complete this sentence with a word from the box.

    This room makes me feel _____.

3. Do you like the room? Why or why not?

> The colors are very bright. They make me feel happy. I like the room.

Word Bank
Opposites (feelings)
relaxed ↔ nervous, uncomfortable
happy ↔ unhappy, sad

C Find another photo of a room in a house. Answer the questions in **B** about it with a partner.

2 LISTENING

A Look up the word *energy* in your dictionary. Then ask a partner: Does your home use a lot of energy?

B Make and check predictions. You will hear a man talk about a "green home." Read the sentence below and guess the answer(s). Then listen and circle the correct answer(s). **Track 24**

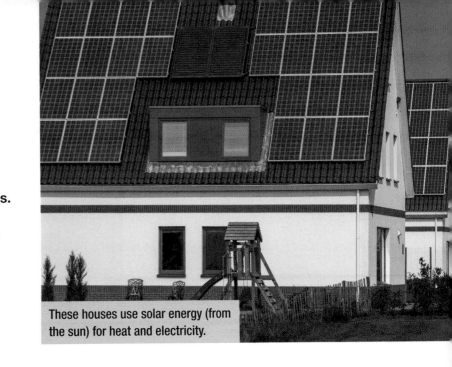
These houses use solar energy (from the sun) for heat and electricity.

A "green home" _____.

    a. saves energy

    b. is the color green

    c. is expensive

    d. is good for the environment (plants, land, water)

C Make predictions. You want your house to be more "green." How can you do it? Look at the photos and read the sentences. Guess the answers with a partner.

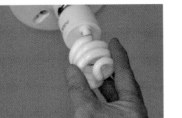

Word Bank
Word partnerships
If you *save energy*, you use less energy.
You can also *save money* and *water*.

1. Unplug your _____, _____, and _____.

2. Use CFL light bulbs. They use _____ energy.

3. When you leave a room, always turn _____ the lights.

4. Take _____-minute showers.

D Listen for details. Listen to the full interview. Complete the sentences in **C**. **Track 25**

E Do you do any of the things in **C** in your house? Tell a partner.

3 ▶ READING 🔊 Track 26

A 🔁 **Make predictions.** Read the title of the article and the question below it. Guess the answers below with a partner. One set of colors is extra.

Room

1. bedroom
2. living room
3. dining room
4. kitchen
5. home office / study room

A good color for the room

a. red, orange, or yellow
b. white only
c. light blue, light green, or light purple
d. white and light blue

B **Check predictions.** Read the passage. Check your answers in **A**.

C **Scan for information.** Complete the chart with the correct colors and feelings.

Room color(s)	Feeling(s)
light blue, light green, or light purple	1. _____
2. _____ _____	alert, sometimes 3. _____, and happy
lots of dark or bright colors	4. _____
5. _____ walls and _____ lights	uncomfortable
6. light _____ and _____	relaxed and ready to study

D 🔁 Answer the questions with a partner. Use ideas from the reading.

1. Look at the photo. Is this room good for studying? relaxing? eating? Why?

2. Answer the questions above about a room in your house.

THE POWER OF COLOR

What are the best colors for rooms in your home?

We see color everywhere. It makes our world beautiful, but it can also affect[1] our feelings and behavior.[2] For this reason, it is important to use the right colors in different rooms in a home. For example, light colors—like light blue, green, or purple—relax us. They are perfect in a bedroom or living room.

Other colors—like red, orange, and yellow— are different. They make us feel alert[3] and sometimes hungry, studies show. For this reason, they can be good to use in a dining area or a kitchen.

A room with some red, orange, or yellow can also feel happy and can be good in a living area. But these colors are very strong,[4] and it's best to only use a little of them. People feel nervous in rooms with too many dark or bright colors.

Other colors help us work or study. Many people think white walls and bright lights are best for this. But people are often uncomfortable in this kind of room. It is hard to sit and think. Instead, use white with another color, especially light blue. This color relaxes people. In a home office or a room for studying, light blue and white can help people think better.

[1] If something *affects* you, it changes you in some way.
[2] Your *behavior* is the way you act.
[3] If you are *alert*, you feel very awake and ready to do things.
[4] A *strong* color is bright or intense.

4 GRAMMAR

A Turn to pages 76–77. Complete the exercises. Then do **B** and **C** below.

	Verb	a / an	very / too	Adjective / Adverb	Noun	to + Verb
				very / too		
This room	is		**very / too**	dark.		
He	talks		**too**	fast. I don't understand.		
I	am		**too**	tired		to watch TV.
They	have	a	**very**	big	house.	

B Write two sentences about each photo with a partner. Use *too* or *very*. Put your sentences on the board.

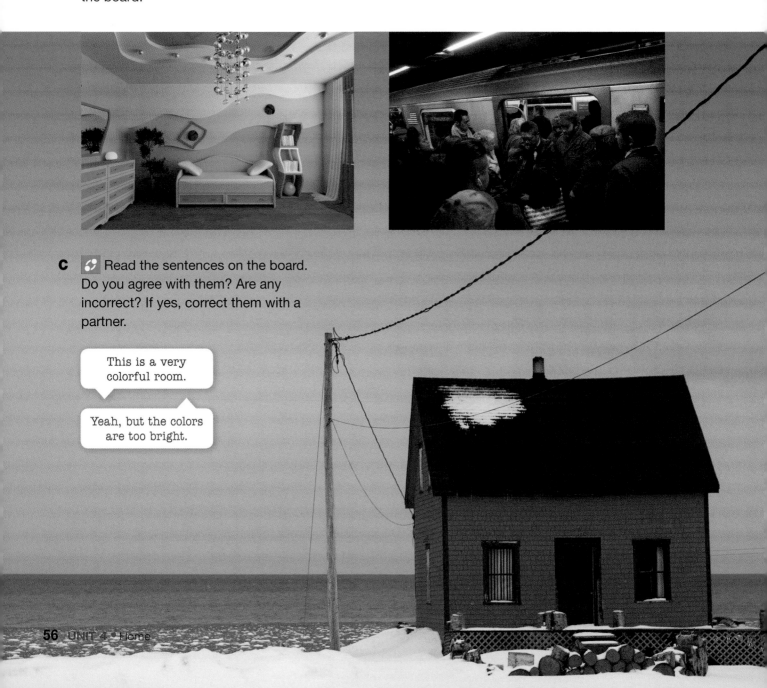

C Read the sentences on the board. Do you agree with them? Are any incorrect? If yes, correct them with a partner.

> This is a very colorful room.

> Yeah, but the colors are too bright.

5 WRITING

A Read about an apartment in Santiago. Then write about your house or apartment.

> I live with my family in an apartment in Santiago. We live on the 6th floor. There are two bedrooms in the apartment. I share one with my sister. In our room, there are two beds, a desk, a bookshelf, and a closet. It's too small for all our clothes! The apartment also has a living room, dining area, a kitchen, and a very big balcony with lots of plants. I like our apartment a lot!

B Share your writing with a partner. Correct any mistakes in his or her writing.

C Return your partner's paper. Then explain: Are your homes similar or different? Give examples.

6 COMMUNICATION

A The TV show *Room Redo* helps a person change a room in his or her home to make it better. Look at the room. Read about this week's person.

B Work with a partner. You work for *Room Redo*. What are the problems with Felix's dorm room? How can you fix these problems? On a piece of paper, list and then draw your ideas.

> The walls are too.... Let's....

C Work with another pair. Explain your ideas to them. When you listen, take notes. What do you like about their ideas?

D Repeat **C** with three other pairs. At the end, review your notes. Then ask a partner: Whose room redo is the best? Why?

Name: Felix Hernandez (male)
Age: 22
Job: Student
His room: Felix lives in a dorm room at City University.

1 STORYBOARD

A Alexis and Peter are at a movie theater. Complete the conversation.

B Get into a group of three. Practice the conversation.

C Change roles and practice the conversation again.

2 SEE IT AND SAY IT

A 🔁 Talk about the photo with a partner.

1. What's the date?

2. What holiday is it?

3. What time is it in the photo? What's happening in the photo?

4. On this holiday, what do you usually do?

B 🔁 Two people at this party are on a date. With a partner, create a dialog between the two people. Role-play your conversation for the class.

3 LISTENING: PHONE MESSAGES

A 🔊 You have four voicemail messages on your phone. Listen. You will hear part of each message. Write the day and date of each call. **Track 27**

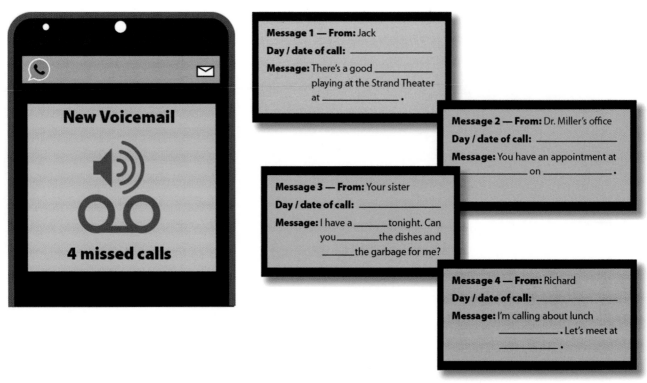

New Voicemail

4 missed calls

Message 1 — From: Jack
Day / date of call: _____
Message: There's a good _____ playing at the Strand Theater at _____ .

Message 2 — From: Dr. Miller's office
Day / date of call: _____
Message: You have an appointment at _____ on _____ .

Message 3 — From: Your sister
Day / date of call: _____
Message: I have a _____ tonight. Can you _____ the dishes and _____ the garbage for me?

Message 4 — From: Richard
Day / date of call: _____
Message: I'm calling about lunch _____ . Let's meet at _____ .

B 🔄 Look at the messages in **A**. Can you guess any of the answers? Tell a partner your ideas.

C 🔊 Listen and complete each phone message in **A**. **Track 28**

D Read your messages. What are the problems with the schedule?

4 WEEKEND ACTIVITIES

A Complete each sentence with your information.

On the weekend, I...

always	usually	often	sometimes	hardly ever	never	
❑	❑	❑	❑	❑	❑	wake up early.
❑	❑	❑	❑	❑	❑	go shopping.
❑	❑	❑	❑	❑	❑	go out with friends.
❑	❑	❑	❑	❑	❑	clean my room.
❑	❑	❑	❑	❑	❑	go on a date.
❑	❑	❑	❑	❑	❑	practice my English.

B 🔄 Compare your answers with a partner's. Ask and answer questions. Are you similar or different?

> Sometimes I wake up early on the weekend.

> What time do you wake up?

> Really? I never wake up early.

> Usually around 10:00 or 11:00. I like to sleep late.

5 PARTY INVITATION

A Look at the invitation below. Then make your own party invitation on a piece of paper. Leave the guest list blank.

Word Bank

have / go to a birthday / dinner / holiday party

You're invited to:

Date:
Friday, May 25
Time:
7:00 to midnight
Place:
The Butterfly Lounge
2501 4th Street

Cleo's Birthday Party

Come and celebrate my 22nd birthday at the Butterfly Lounge. The food, music, and drinks are free!

Guest List:

Kathy	Maria & Carlos
Yu Kim	Kenichi
Marithe	Yang & Jenny

B Put your invitation on the classroom wall. Read the other invitations.

• Which parties are interesting to you? Write your name on the guest list.

• Write information about your party choices on a piece of paper.

C 🔄 Tell a partner about your party choices. Why do you want to go to these parties?

> Let's go to Cleo's birthday party on Friday night. The Butterfly Lounge is fun, and the food and drinks are free.

> Great idea! Let's go together.

6 STORYBOARD

A Gary and Mina are at a party. Eun Mi and Carlos are shopping in Mexico City. Complete the two conversations.

Conversation 1: Gary and Mina **Conversation 2: Eun Mi and Carlos**

_____ ?

That's Luis. He's my brother's friend.

Hey, Carlos, what does that sign say? I _____ read it.

REBAJAS de VERANO

It says "Summer Sale." Let's go inside.

What's _____ ?

He's a really outgoing guy.

This is a nice jacket. How _____ ?

It's 570 pesos.

What _____ ?

He's a delivery _____. He _____ DHL Global Mail.

_____ that in Korean won?

It's about _____ won.

B 🔁 Practice the conversations with a partner.

C 🔁 Change roles and practice again.

7 SEE IT AND SAY IT

A 🔄 Study the picture. Take turns answering the questions with a partner.

1. What things are in the picture?

2. Look at the people in the picture. What are they wearing?

B 🔄 What are the people in the photo saying? Create a conversation with a partner.

> Excuse me. How much is that sofa?

> It's $2,000.

> Oh, that's too expensive!

8 SPOT THE DIFFERENCES

A Look at the two pictures. What are the people doing? What are they wearing? What colors are the items? With a partner, find as many differences between the two pictures as you can in five minutes.

B How many did you see? Compare your ideas with another pair.

9 JOB ADS

A Look at the job ads. Can you do these jobs? Tell your partner.

> I can do the receptionist job.
> I can type quickly and...

Sundance Studio needs an outgoing dance teacher!

Teach children to dance

You: Friendly and outgoing dance teacher. Work well with children ages 6-8.

Days and hours: Thursday, Friday, and Saturday part-time, 5-9 PM.

Pay: $35 per hour

Wanted: Friendly, hardworking receptionist for an international office

You: Type quickly
Speak English on the phone
It helps if you can speak one of these languages: Chinese, Japanese, Korean, Portuguese, Russian, Spanish, or Thai.

Days and hours: Monday – Friday 8 AM – 5 PM.

Pay: $28,000 per year

B Now make your own job ad on a piece of paper. Write the name of the job, the responsibilities and requirements, the days and hours, and the pay.

C Put your ad on the classroom wall. Read the other ads. Which jobs can you do? Make a list.

D Tell a partner about the jobs on your list. Which jobs are good for you? Why?

10 WHAT DO YOU DO?

A 🔁 **Predict.** Look at the photos. Can you guess any information in the chart? Work with a partner.

Name	Job	Where	What's the job like?	Wants to...
Bill	_____	at a place called The Matrix	works _____	have his own _____ restaurant
Kira	works for herself	has a _____ store online	great, but she's _____ busy	get someone to _____ her
Juan	_____	in _____	sometimes _____	work during the _____
Diya	is doing an internship as a _____	at a tech company	interesting	get a _____ job there

B 🔊 **Listen for details.** Listen. Complete the chart above with the correct word(s). **Track 29**

C 🔁 Answer the questions. Then ask a partner four *Wh-* questions of your own about the people.

1. What does Bill do?
2. Where does Juan work?
3. Who works for herself?
4. What is Juan's job like?
5. Who works a lot?
6. In the future, what does Diya want to do?

D 🔁 Work with a partner. Make a dialog between two people in the photos. Use the notes in the chart and your own ideas. Try to talk for two minutes.

> So, what do you do, Bill?

> I'm a chef.

> What's that like?

> It's interesting, but I have to work a lot.

LESSON A

Vocabulary

beans
bread
cheese
coffee
(fried) chicken
eggs
fish
fruit
(orange) juice
meat
milk
onions
pasta
(baked) potato
rice
(spinach) salad
(tuna) sandwich
soda
(vegetable) soup
spaghetti
steak
tea
tomato (sauce)
vegetable

breakfast
lunch
dinner

hungry
meal

Speaking Strategy

Talking about likes and dislikes
Do you like (Indian) food?
Do you like (fish)?

Yes! I love it!
Yes, I like it a lot.
Yeah, it's OK.
No, not really.
No, I can't stand it.

LESSON B

Vocabulary

bananas
cancer
(a) cold
energy
good for you ↔ bad for you
have / eat breakfast
healthy ↔ unhealthy
high (in) ↔ low (in) (calories /
   sugar / protein)
honey
ice
ice cream
illness
junk food
medicine
milk
oranges
skin
skip (breakfast)
snack
stomach
strawberries
taste good ↔ taste bad
vitamins
yogurt

UNIT 2 TIME

LESSON A

Vocabulary

wake up
take a shower
get dressed
leave home
start (class)
finish (class)
study
go home
do homework
go to bed

two (o'clock)
two-oh-five / five after two
two fifteen / quarter after two
two thirty / half past two
two forty-five / quarter to three
two fifty-five / five to three

in the morning / afternoon / evening
at noon / midnight
at night

yesterday / today / tonight / tomorrow

early / late

Speaking Strategy

Making suggestions
Let's see a movie.
We could see a movie.

Saying *yes*
(That) sounds good.
Good / Great idea.

Saying *no* politely
I don't really like French food.
I don't really want to see that movie.

LESSON B

Vocabulary

(a) day off
go dancing, shopping
go for a walk, bike ride, run
go out with friends, family, your boyfriend or girlfriend
go to the movies, gym, beach, a club, concert, party, friend's house
(on) the weekend
spend time with (someone)

UNIT 3 SPECIAL OCCASIONS

LESSON A

Vocabulary

January
February
March
April
May
June
July
August
September
October
November
December

ordinal numbers: first, second, third, fourth, etc.

When were you born?
 I was born…

spring, summer, fall / autumn, winter

Speaking Strategy

Saying you know or don't know something
Is tomorrow a holiday?
 Yes, it is. / No, it isn't.
 I'm not sure. It could be.
 I don't (really) know.
When is Labor Day?
 It's on September 3rd this year.
 I'm not sure. Is it in September?
 I don't (really) know.

LESSON B

Vocabulary

annual
attend
celebrate
compete
event
festival (art, film, food, holiday, music, sport, spring, summer, autumn, winter)
miss
parade
perform
take photos
take place
traditional

Saying how often something happens
daily, weekly, monthly, annually
every two / three / four years

LESSON A

Vocabulary

air conditioner (A/C)
balcony
bathroom
bed
bedroom
chair
closet
dining room
elevator
garage
kitchen
lamp
living room
oven
refrigerator
rent
rug
shower
sink
sofa
stairs
table
toilet
wall
window
yard

Speaking Strategy

Showing surprise

My house has 20 rooms.
  Really? / Are you serious? / For
  real?
Yeah.

My house has 20 rooms.
  You're kidding. / You're joking. /
  No way.
(No,) it's true.

LESSON B

Vocabulary

Colors
black
(dark / light) blue
brown
gray
green
orange
pink
purple
red
white
(bright) yellow

Feelings
relaxed ↔ nervous,
  uncomfortable
happy ↔ unhappy, sad

save energy / water / money
turn on ↔ turn off the TV, the
  lights, the A/C

UNIT 1 FOOD

LESSON A

The Simple Present Tense: Affirmative Statements		
Subject pronoun	**Verb**	
I / You / We / They	eat	meat.
He / She / It	eats	

The Simple Present Tense: Negative Statements					Contractions with *do*
Subject pronoun	***do***	***not***	**Verb**		
I / You / We / They	**do**	(not)	eat	meat.	do not = don't
He / She / It	**does**				does not = doesn't

Spelling rules for third person singular (*he, she, it*)

In most cases, add *s* to the base form of the verb: *eat → eat**s***

If the base form ends in *s, sh, ch, x, or z,* add *es*: *tea**ch** → teach**es***

If the base form ends in consonant + *y,* change the *y* to *i* and add *es*: *stud**y** → stud**ies***

If the base form ends in consonant + *o,* add *es*: *g**o** → g**oes**   d**o** → d**oes***

The verb *have* is irregular: *have → **has***

A   Complete the sentences. Use the simple present tense.

1. Maria (live) _____ in Barcelona, but her parents (live) _____ in a small town. Of course, she (speak) _____ Spanish. She also (understand) _____ some French, but she (not / speak) _____ it well.

2. Duncan (teach) _____ at a cooking school. Sarah (go) _____ to school there, and she (enjoy) _____ it. School (finish) _____ at 3:00. After school, Sarah (hurry) _____ from campus to her part-time job. She (work) _____ in a restaurant.

3. In my family, we (not / use) _____ a fork and knife. We (use) _____ chopsticks to eat our meals. We (have) _____ rice every day. My little brother (have) _____ milk every morning. My mother (not / drink) _____ milk. She (drink) _____ coffee every morning.

B   ♻ Rewrite the information in **A** (item 3) above so that it is true for you and your family. Then share it with a partner.

LESSON B

Simple Present *Yes* / *No* Questions					
do	Subject	Verb		Short answers	Contractions with *do*
Do	you	like	spicy food?	Yes, I do. / No, I don't.	do not = don't
Does	he / she			Yes, he / she does. / No, he / she doesn't.	does not = doesn't
Do	you			Yes, we do. / No, we don't.	do not = don't
	they			Yes, they do. / No, they don't.	

A Complete the questions and answers.

1. __Do__ you like spicy food?   No, _____.

2. _____ they speak English?   Yes, _____.

3. _____ he have breakfast every day?   No, _____.

4. _____ we have a test today?   Yes, _____.

5. _____ your mother cook well?   Yes, _____.

6. _____ you and your boyfriend eat lunch together? No, _____.

B Complete the dialogs with *Yes* / *No* questions and answers. Then practice with a partner.

1. A: What are you eating?

   B: Pasta with chocolate sauce.

   A: Really? (it / taste) _____ good?

   B: Yes, _____. (you / want) _____ some?

2. A: (you / know) _____ Jamie Oliver?

   B: No, _____. Who is he?

   A: He's a famous chef from England.

   B: Oh yeah! (he / have) _____ a show on TV?

   A: _____. It's on Channel 4.

3. A: My parents want to go to a nice restaurant. (you / know) _____ a good place?

   B: (they / like) _____ spicy food?

   A: Yeah, my dad _____, but my mom _____.

   B: Oh, okay. Well, (they / eat) _____ sushi?

   A: _____. They love it.

   B: Try Umami Sushi. It's a good place.

C Write short answers to the questions on a piece of paper. Then compare your answers with a partner's.

1. Do you want to try the pasta with chocolate sauce?

2. Do you know Jamie Oliver or other famous chefs?

3. Do your parents like spicy food? How about sushi? Do you?

UNIT 2 TIME

LESSON A

Prepositions of Time		
When is your class?	It's **on** Monday. 　　**on** Mondays. (every Monday) 　　**on** Tuesday night.	day of the week
	It's **in** the morning / afternoon / evening. It's **at** night.	period of the day
	It's **at** 8:30. 　　**at** noon.	specific time
	It's **from** 4:00 **to** 5:30. 　　**from** Tuesday **to** Saturday.	length of time (start to finish)

A Read about Lucia's schedule. Fill in the blanks with *in, on, at, from,* or *to.*

1. My name is Lucia. I'm a nurse. I work _____ Monday _____ Friday.

2. I work in the hospital _____ night. My shift is _____ midnight _____ 9:30 _____ the morning.

3. On workdays, I go to bed _____ 3 PM and wake up _____ 10 PM.

4. I do my grocery shopping _____ the afternoon and _____ Saturdays.

5. It's difficult because my husband works _____ 9 AM _____ 6 PM every day. I don't see him a lot.

6. _____ Sundays, we are both off. We like to go to the park together and relax.

B 🗨 What do you think of Lucia's schedule? Tell a partner.

C 🗨 Think of another night job. Answer the questions about the job. Look online to learn more. Then tell a partner.

1. Which days do you work in this job? _____

2. What time does the job start and finish? _____

3. Is the job easy or difficult? _____

LESSON B

Simple Present *Wh-* Questions				
Question word	**do / does**	**Subject**	**Verb**	**Answers**
Who	do	you	study with?	(I study with) Maria.
What	does	she	do on Saturdays?	(She) goes out with friends.
When	do	they	have class?	(They have class) at 8:00.
		we		(We have class) on Mondays.
Where	does	he		(He has class) in Room 3B.

A Read each item. Then use the words in parentheses and information in the responses to complete the questions.

1. A: Who (you) _____ *do you live* _____ with?
   B: I live with my sister.

2. A: When (your brother) _____ in the morning?
   B: He wakes up at 7:15.

3. A: Where (your grandparents) _____?
   B: They live in London.

4. A: What time (this class) _____?
   B: It ends at 2:30.

5. A: When (we) _____ a test in this class?
   B: We have a test tomorrow.

6. A: What (you) _____ on the weekends?
   B: I go out with my friends.

B 🔲 Ask a partner the questions in **A**.

UNIT **3** SPECIAL OCCASIONS

LESSON A

Prepositions of Time: *in* and *on*		
When is the holiday party?	It's **on** December 20th. It's **on** Christmas Eve. It's **on** Monday.	Use *on* before days of the week, dates, and holidays.
	It's **in** the morning / afternoon / evening. It's **in** December. It's **in** the winter. It's **in** (early / late) 2016.	Use *in* before times of day, months, seasons, and years.

A Complete these sentences with the correct prepositions.

1. In my city, schools are closed _____ Christmas Day. This year, Christmas is _____ Thursday so we have Friday off, too!

   In my family, we get up _____ the morning and open presents. We have a big holiday meal _____ the afternoon. It's a fun day!

2. The Olympics are _____ the summer and _____ the winter. _____ 2020, the Summer Olympics are in Tokyo. They begin _____ July 24th. _____ 2018, the Winter Olympics are in South Korea. They begin _____ February.

3. Many countries have Father's Day _____ the third Sunday _____ June. _____ Father's Day in Venezuela, families come together and have lunch.

When and How long Questions		
With be	**When** is the festival?	It's **in** July / **on** Thursday. It starts **on** July 1 / **at** 10:00.
	How long is the festival?	(It's) **from** July 1 **to** July 3. (It lasts) **until** July 3. **for** three days.
With other verbs	**When** do you study?	(I study) **on** Saturdays / **in** the evening.
	How long do you study?	(I study) **from** 4:00 **to** 6:00. **until** 6:00. **for** an hour.

A *When* question usually asks for specific time information—a specific day, month, or time of day. But sometimes, it can ask about a length of time. For example, it's possible to ask "When is the festival?" and answer "It's from July 1 to 3."
How long only asks about a length of time.

A Circle the correct words in the dialogs. There may be more than one correct answer. Then practice them with a partner.

1. A: When / How long do you work today?
   B: From / For / To 4:00 for / to / at 8:00.

2. A: When / How long is our holiday break?
   B: It starts in / on / at the ninth.

3. A: When / How long are you staying in London?
   B: Until / For / To January third.

4. A: When / How long does vacation last?
   B: From / Until / For a month.

B Complete each dialog with a *When* or *How long* question, or an answer.

Event	Dates
Summer break	June 19–September 19
The school festival	April 1–7
Department store holiday hours	Every day, 8:00 AM–midnight

1. A: When does summer break start?
   B: _____

2. A: _____
   B: Summer break lasts for three months.

3. A: _____
   B: It ends on April 7.

4. A: _____
   B: The festival lasts _____.

5. A: _____

   B: The department store opens _____.

6. A: How late is the store open?

   B: _____

7. A: How long is the store open every day?

   B: _____

UNIT 4 HOME

LESSON A

There is / There are				
There is / isn't			**Singular noun**	
There is (There's)	a / an one		chair / air conditioner closet	in my bedroom.
There is **There isn't**	no a / an		balcony garage / elevator	in my building.
There are / aren't			**Plural noun**	
There are	— / four / some / many			
There are **There aren't**	no any		elevators	in that building.

Use *there is / there are* to say that something does or doesn't exist, or to say its location.
there's is the contracted form of *there is*. *There are* does not have a contracted form.

Questions	Short answers
Is there an elevator in your building?	Yes, **there is**. / No, **there isn't**.
Are there (any) windows in your living room?	Yes, **there are**. / No, **there aren't** (any).
How many windows **are (there)** in your bedroom?	**There's** one. / **There are** two. / **There aren't** any.

A Read about the Winchester Mystery House. Complete the sentences with *there's, there isn't, there are,* or *there aren't.*

(1.) _____ a big, strange house in California: the Winchester Mystery

House. (2.) _____ about 160 rooms in the house, including 40 bedrooms,

and (3.) _____ three elevators. (4.) _____ stairs and doors that go

nowhere. (5.) _____ a special room in the house. (6.) _____ only

one door that goes into the room, but (7.) _____ three doors that exit it.

(8.) _____ a beautiful garden and a large bell. Many tourists visit the house.

(9.) _____ tours during the day, but (10.) _____ any tours at night.

(11.) _____ an easy way to get out—so be careful! Don't get lost!

B  Complete the questions about the Winchester Mystery House. Then ask and answer them with a partner.

1. _____ rooms are there in the house?

2. _____ any elevators?

3. _____ bedrooms are there?

4. _____ a garden?

5. _____ bells are there?

6. _____ tours at night?

LESSON B

				very / too			
	Verb	**a / an**	**very / too**	**Adjective / Adverb**	**Noun**	**to + Verb**
❶ This room	is		**very / too**	dark.		
❷ He	talks		**too**	fast. I don't understand.		
❸ I	am		**too**	tired		to watch TV.
❹ They	have	a	**very**	big	house.	

❶ *Very* and *too* make adjectives and adverbs stronger.

❷ Use *too* when something is more than you need or want and there is <u>a negative result</u>.
   ☞He talks **too** fast. <u>I can't understand him</u>. / This room is **too** dark, and <u>I can't see</u>.

❸ Use *too* with this pattern (*too* + verb).
   ☞I'm **too tired to watch** TV. I'm going to bed.

❹ Use *very* to modify an adjective + noun: *They have a **very big house**.*
   Don't use *too*: ~~They have a too big house.~~

A Complete the sentences with *very* or *too.*

1. It's _____ noisy in here. I can't hear you. Let's go outside.
2. This is a _____ beautiful color. Let's use it in the dining room.
3. These chairs are _____ old, but we can still use them.
4. This dorm room is _____ small for four people. Four students can't live in here.
5. My neighbor is a _____ nice person. I like him a lot.
6. We're _____ late for the movie. It started at 7:00, and now it's 8:20. It's almost over.
7. He lives in a _____ large apartment; it's almost 400 square meters!
8. I'm _____ tired to walk to the fifth floor. I'm taking the elevator.
9. The rent here is $1,000 a month. That's _____ expensive for me. I can only pay $800.
10. These apartments are _____ expensive, but a lot of people buy them.

B 🌐 Complete the sentences with *very* or *too* and your ideas. Then explain your answers to a partner.

1. My bedroom is _____.
2. I'm too old to _____.
3. I'm too young to _____.
4. English is _____.
5. Right now, it's _____ early to _____.

ADDITIONAL GRAMMAR NOTES

Possessive Nouns		
Singular nouns (+ 's)	Plural nouns (+ ')	Irregular plural nouns (+ 's)
sister → sister's brother → brother's	parents → parents' brothers → brothers'	children → children's women → women's

For first and last names that end in *s*, you can add **'s** or just **'**.

A Look up the word *twin* in a dictionary. Read about Hallie Parker and Annie James from the movie *The Parent Trap.* Complete the sentences with a singular noun, a plural noun, or a possessive noun.

1. Hallie Parker lives in her (father) _____ home in California, in the US.

2. Annie (James) _____ home is in London. She lives there with her (mother) _____.

3. The two (girl) _____, Hallie and Annie, are (twin) _____! But they live apart. They don't know about each other.

4. (Hallie) _____ summer plans are exciting. She's going to summer camp. And by chance, (Annie) _____ is going to the same summer camp!

5. At camp, Hallie sees her (sister) _____ face for the first time. They look the same! They are both surprised and happy.

6. Hallie doesn't know her (mom) _____ name, and Annie doesn't know her (dad) _____ name.

7. Before the two (child) _____ leave camp, they have an idea. The two (sister) _____ plan is an exciting one!

B 🔁 What do you think happens next? Write three sentences. Tell your partner.

_____.

_____.

_____.

	Possessive Adjectives	Possessive Pronouns	*belong to*
Whose passable is this?	It's **my** passport.	It's **mine.**	It **belongs to me.**
	your	yours.	you.
	her	hers.	her.
	his	his.	him.
	our	ours.	us.
	their	theirs.	them.

Whose and *who's* have the same pronunciation but different meanings.

Whose asks about the owner of something: *Whose house is that? It's mine.*

Who's is a contraction of *Who* and *is*: *Who's studying English? Maria is.*

A Write the correct possessive pronoun for the underlined words.

1. A: That's not her suitcase.

   B: No, <ins>her suitcase</ins> is over there.
   (hers)

2. A: Can I use your cell phone? <ins>My cell phone</ins> doesn't work.

   B: Sorry, but I forgot my cell phone at home. Use <ins>Jon's phone</ins>.

3. A: Is your class fun?

   B: Yes, but <ins>Aya and Leo's class</ins> is more interesting.

4. A: Is your hometown hot in the summer? <ins>My hometown</ins> is.

   B: <ins>Our hometown</ins> is, too.

5. A: Your birthday is in May.

   B: That's right, and <ins>your birthday</ins> is in March.

B 🔄 Use the words in the chart to complete the conversation. Then practice the dialog with a partner.

JIM: Well, I have (1.) _____my_____ luggage. Where's
(2.) _____ ?

BEN: Um... let's see... oh, here's (3.) _____
suitcase. No, wait... this one isn't (4.) _____.

JIM: (5.) _____ is it?

BEN: It says Mr. Simon Konig. It belongs to
(6.) _____.

JIM: Hey, I think that man has (7.) _____
suitcase. See? He probably thinks it's
(8.) _____.

BEN: I'll ask him. Excuse me, does this suitcase
belong to (9.) _____ ?

SIMON: Oh, sorry. My mistake! I thought it was (10.) _____!

↓ LUGGAGE

Answers

Speaking page 35, C

1. c **2.** b **3.** c **4.** a

NOTES

NOTES

NOTES

NOTES

NOTES